Lessons of Love Through Time
Book 1

The Beginning of Lies

Written and Illustrated by

Melinda Hindley

World rights reserved. This book or any portion thereof may not be copied or reproduced in any form or manner whatever, except as provided by law, without the written permission of the publisher, except by a reviewer who may quote brief passages in a review.

The author assumes full responsibility for the accuracy of all facts and quotations as cited in this book. The opinions expressed in this book are the author's personal views and interpretations, and do not necessarily reflect those of the publisher.

This book is provided with the understanding that the publisher is not engaged in giving spiritual, legal, medical, or other professional advice. If authoritative advice is needed, the reader should seek the counsel of a competent professional.

Copyright © 2018 Melinda Hindley
Copyright © 2018 TEACH Services, Inc.
ISBN-13: 978-1-4796-0982-6 (Paperback)
ISBN-13: 978-1-4796-0984-0 (Hardback)
ISBN-13: 978-1-4796-0983-3 (ePub)
Library of Congress Control Number: 2018956437

Dedication

To the One who keeps on loving me.
For the little ones and the important questions they ask.

Special thanks to my son Kenneth for technical support, and to my daughter Helen for running the household so I could enter deeply into "Book Mode!"

Foreword

Children have questions, and questions are important. Have you ever wondered...
Where did bad come from?
Why did God put a bad tree in the garden?
Why did God want people to make little lambs die?
Did God get mad and drown people for being bad?
Where does sad come from?

These questions are very important.
These are the questions of the great controversy.
God wants us to know that He REALLY does love us.
Satan wants us to think that God doesn't REALLY love us.

Sometimes Bible stories are hard to understand.
Sometimes things in life are hard to understand.
How we understand these things will decide who we believe.

Big Issues Without Big Words

Table of Contents

Chapter 1   The First Bad, The First Sad. 6

Chapter 2   God Makes a Special Home 17

Chapter 3   God Makes a Special Family. 23

Chapter 4   God Makes a Special Day 29

Chapter 5   A Warning. 37

Chapter 6   Eve Tries to Be Smart 43

Chapter 7   Poison Seeds 49

Chapter 8   God Comes to Visit. 55

Chapter 9   God Has a Plan 60

Chapter 10   Adam and Eve Learn About the Lamb 68

Chapter 11   Cain and the Lamb 78

Chapter 12   Dangerous Thoughts 84

Chapter 13   Dangerous Choosing 93

Chapter 14   Noah Helps 100

Chapter 15   God Looks Away 107

Chapter 16   A Bad, Bad Trick 116

CHAPTER 1
The First Bad, The First Sad

Long, long ago, before God made anything,
   there was God.
God was made up of three, but you could only see two.
Everything that God thought was true and loving.
Everything that God did was loving and right.
That's why there had never been a bad,
   And there had never been a sad.

God was happy.

"Let's build a pretty universe," They said.

Then They wanted to share even more.

They decided to make friends who could love and be happy too.

So, up, up high, past the sky,

They made lots and lots of angels to live with Them in heaven.

The angels were bright and shiny,
    One angel was the shiniest.
The angels were close to God.
    One angel was the closest.
The angels sang and sang.
    One angel sang the best.
The angels were very, very happy.
    But one angel was not happy.
Why?

The angels loved Jesus best.
One angel loved himself best.
His name was Lucifer.
He said, "I am the shiniest angel.
I sing the best.
I wish the angels did not love Jesus best.
The angels need to love me best."
But Lucifer did not say that out loud.
Oh, no!

He told all the angels,
"I know God the best. God is not on your side.
God is not fair.
His rules don't make you happy."
The angels did not know what to think.

God went to talk to Lucifer.

"I love you," God said.

"My rules help everyone be happy."

Lucifer knew that God was right,

But Lucifer did not say that out loud.

Oh, no!

He told God, "All the angels are on my side."

God said, "Some angels think that you are right.

Some angels know that I love them.

Some angels do not know what to believe."

Lucifer and his angels stopped following God's rules.
They became angry and did not want to love each other.
   That was the first bad.
Lucifer and his angels stopped believing that God loved them.
Then they did not want to love God.
   That was the first sad.

God was sad.
He said, "Lucifer, your name means that you are
 a special messenger that tells the truth[1].
But you are not telling the truth anymore.
Because you have chosen to tell lies, your name is now going to be Satan."

---

[1] "Lucifer" means light-bearer, but what does that mean? "Light" is a word that we use to describe truth. "Bearer" is someone who carries a message.

Satan said, "I am not going to follow Your rules! I am not going to stay here. I am not happy here anymore. The angels on my side are not happy here anymore. We are going to go away."
All the unhappy angels went away.

Now they try to make us unhappy.
They say, "God is not on your side.
    God is not fair.
    His rules don't make you happy."
They tell God, "All the people are on our side."
God says, "Some people think that you are right.
    Some people know that I love them.
    Some people do not know what to believe."

We can choose.
We do not have to be angry.
We can believe that His rules help us to be happy.
We can love each other.
We can know that God loves us, and we can love God too.
Then we will be very, very happy.
Then God will be happy, too.

CHAPTER 2
God Makes a Special Home

Long, long ago God came to see Earth.
It was empty and dark.
God did not want Earth to be dark.
"Let there be light!" He said.

He put the light over here.
He put the dark over there.
That was the first evening.
That morning and evening made day one.
God said, "That is good!"

The next day, God came to see Earth.
It did not have any shape.
God did not want Earth to be all mixed up.
"Let there be sky!" He said.

He put some of the water over here.
He put some of the water over there.
He put the air in between.
That evening and morning made day two.
God said, "That is good!"

The next day, God came to see Earth.
It was full of water.
God did not want Earth to be all wet.
"Let there be dry land!" He said.

He put the water over here.
He put the dirt over there.
"Now," He said, "Let there be plants!"
Trees and grass and flowers grew on the dirt.
Reeds and seaweed and lily-pads grew on the water.
That evening and morning made day three.
God said, "That is good!"

The next day, God came to see Earth.
It was in a spot all by itself.
God did not want Earth to be alone.
"Let there be a solar system!" He said.

He put the moon over here.
He put the sun over there.
He put the planets here and there.
They all went 'round and 'round.
That evening and morning made day four.
God said, "That is good!"

The next day, God came
to see Earth.
It was very still and quiet.
God did not want Earth
to be without songs.
"Let there be singers!"
He said.

He put the birds over here.
They sang songs in the sky.
He put the whales over there.
They sang songs in the water.
Every one sang a different song.
That evening and morning
made day five.
God said, "That is good!"

The next day, God came to see Earth.
There were friends in the sky.
There were friends in the water.
But nothing bounded through the meadows.
Nothing crawled around the pebbles.
"Let there be land animals!" He said.
Now there were friends everywhere.

Then God smiled.
"It's ready, and I'm ready," He said.
"I'm ready for my extra special friends,
 and their home is ready too."

CHAPTER 3
God Makes a Special Family

It was still day six.
Everything was ready for God's extra special friends.
But where were they?

God put His fingers into the mud by the river.
Very carefully He put the head over here.
He put the arms and legs over there.
He added His Spirit as a special gift.
He had made a man. Adam was alive!

Adam was full of energy!
Adam was full of ideas!
But Adam was all alone.
He was the only person.
God said, "That is NOT good!"

God knew that Adam needed someone very special to share with.
Adam agreed to share a part of himself,
and God took it and used it to help make another person.

This person was different. She was a woman.
Her name was Eve.
But she was the same.
Eve was full of energy!
Eve was full of ideas!
And she had the special gift of God's Spirit too.

God brought Eve to Adam.
"Love makes both of you together into one family!"
   He said.
"This is a special picture that will help you
   understand about the three of Us that is God.
When a man and a woman become a family, they will
   want to share more and more too, just like God.
In My plan, the special love that you have for each
   other will create children."
This is a special picture of God too!

Both Adam and Eve had beautiful light clothes.
Both of them loved God.
Both of them loved the special earth home that God had made.
Adam and Eve loved each other too.

God told them to take good care of the whole earth home
　　that He had made for them.
Then He showed them the special place where He had built their
　　special garden home.
Their special job was to work to make their garden pretty and fun.

CHAPTER 4
God Makes a Special Day

The next day, God came to see His friends.
Adam and Eve were waiting!
What was going to make this day so special?

"Today is the very special day!" God said.

"Today is day seven!

"Today, all My work in making your special home is finished.

"All My work in making a family is finished."

"Today I want to spend time with you!"

"All day!"

"That's why I want you to not work today, too."

"My plan is that we can spend the whole day together every time it's day seven."

Adam and Eve were so happy!
What a special day!
They could spend the whole day with God!
They could do it again every week!
They loved God!
What good gifts He had given them!
And day seven was the best gift of all!

They could spend the whole day remembering
when God had made the beautiful Earth.
And when He had said, "That is good!"

They could spend the whole day remembering
when God had made their family.
And when He had said, "That is VERY good!"

They could spend the whole day learning more
about how wonderful God is!

God is happy that you are His special friend too.
God still remembers every time it's day seven.
He wants you to remember too,
  so He can come and spend the whole day with you.
Day seven is so special!
Remembering to spend that time with God makes us so happy.
Spending time with each other is an important way that we show love.

But someone is not happy!
Remember when Satan was still in heaven?
What did he say when the angels loved God best?

What did he say out loud?

Satan still tells lies about God.
He still tells lies about God's laws.
He tries to keep us too busy to remember day seven.
He tries to tell us that day seven isn't important.

Remember the Sabbath day
and keep it a special time.
Set it aside for God.

Six days you should do all your work,
but day seven is different, and you need
to stop working.

That includes you and your whole family,
and anybody who works for you,
and any animals that belong to you,
and anybody who is visiting you.

Because for six days God worked
    making the sky
    and the ground
    and the ocean,
    and everything that lives there.
Six days is what He gives us to work too.

Day seven was the day that God rested.
Day seven is the day God has given us to
    rest too.

He put a special blessing on the rest day,
    so when we remember it we are
    even happier!
He set it apart as a special present.

Exodus 20:8-11

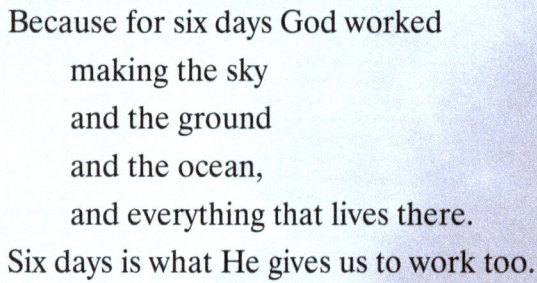

CHAPTER 5
A Warning

Adam and Eve were the very first people that lived on earth.
Nothing had ever died.
Not even one leaf had turned brown.
God had carefully made them.
He carefully made a special garden with a wall around it
    to be a special home for them.
He planted trees in it that were full of the yummiest fruit.
He came to visit them every evening and every Sabbath day.

Angels came to visit too, so Adam and Eve had lots of friends.

Satan and his angels wanted to talk to them, too.
They told God, "You are not being fair.
  We need a chance to talk to Adam and Eve too."

God said, "Your lies are poison seeds,
but I will let you have one spot where you can talk to them."

So God made two very special trees and put them in the special garden. One tree He called "the tree of life" because when Adam and Eve chose to eat that fruit, it was a special sign that they knew that God loved them.

The other tree He called "the tree of knowing both good and evil." That was the spot where Satan could talk to them. Eating that fruit would show that they no longer believed that God loved them. If they chose to think like that even one time, it would be a poison seed inside them that would grow and kill them.

Oh, how God wanted His friends to stay alive and happy forever! He talked to Adam and Eve very seriously.

"Please don't listen to Satan
    at the tree of knowing good and evil.
Be careful not to eat that fruit,
    because the seeds of that way of thinking will kill you.
If you stay together, you can help each other."

Angels came and cried,
"Please don't eat the fruit!"
"Of course we won't," Adam and Eve promised.
"We know that God really loves us."

CHAPTER 6
Eve Tries to Be Smart

One day, as Adam and Eve were enjoying their garden, Eve suddenly noticed that she couldn't see Adam anymore. "I better go find him," she thought, but then she had another thought. "I am really just as smart as Adam. I don't really need to stay so close."

Then she noticed something else.
    There it was!
That one tree that had fruit that she wasn't supposed to eat.
    How pretty it was!
She walked a little closer.
    How strange!
Why had God said to stay away from it?

"Did God really tell you not to eat this yummy fruit?"
    Who said that?
    It sounded a lot like what she had just been thinking!
She walked a little closer to see.

The only someone there was one of those beautiful snakes that had shiny wings. But everyone knows that animals can't talk, even if they are shiny.
"You are so beautiful!"
It was the snake! What nice things it was saying!

"You know, I can talk now because I ate this fruit!
It isn't poison at all, so you definitely won't die like God said.
    And it is so very yummy!
God knows that if you had some, you would be as smart as
He is. After all, it is called 'the tree of knowing good and evil.'
I bet God doesn't want that to happen.
That's why He said not to eat it.
    And it is so very yummy!"

The fruit did look yummy!
The snake was eating it.
He wasn't dead at all.
He could even talk to her.

Eve wanted to eat that yummy fruit.
She wanted to be as smart as God.
She decided to believe the snake.

It was very yummy!
She felt different too.
Maybe this is what being as smart as God feels like.
It didn't feel like something as terrible as dying.
She picked a bunch more.
Quick! She needed to go tell Adam all she had learned!

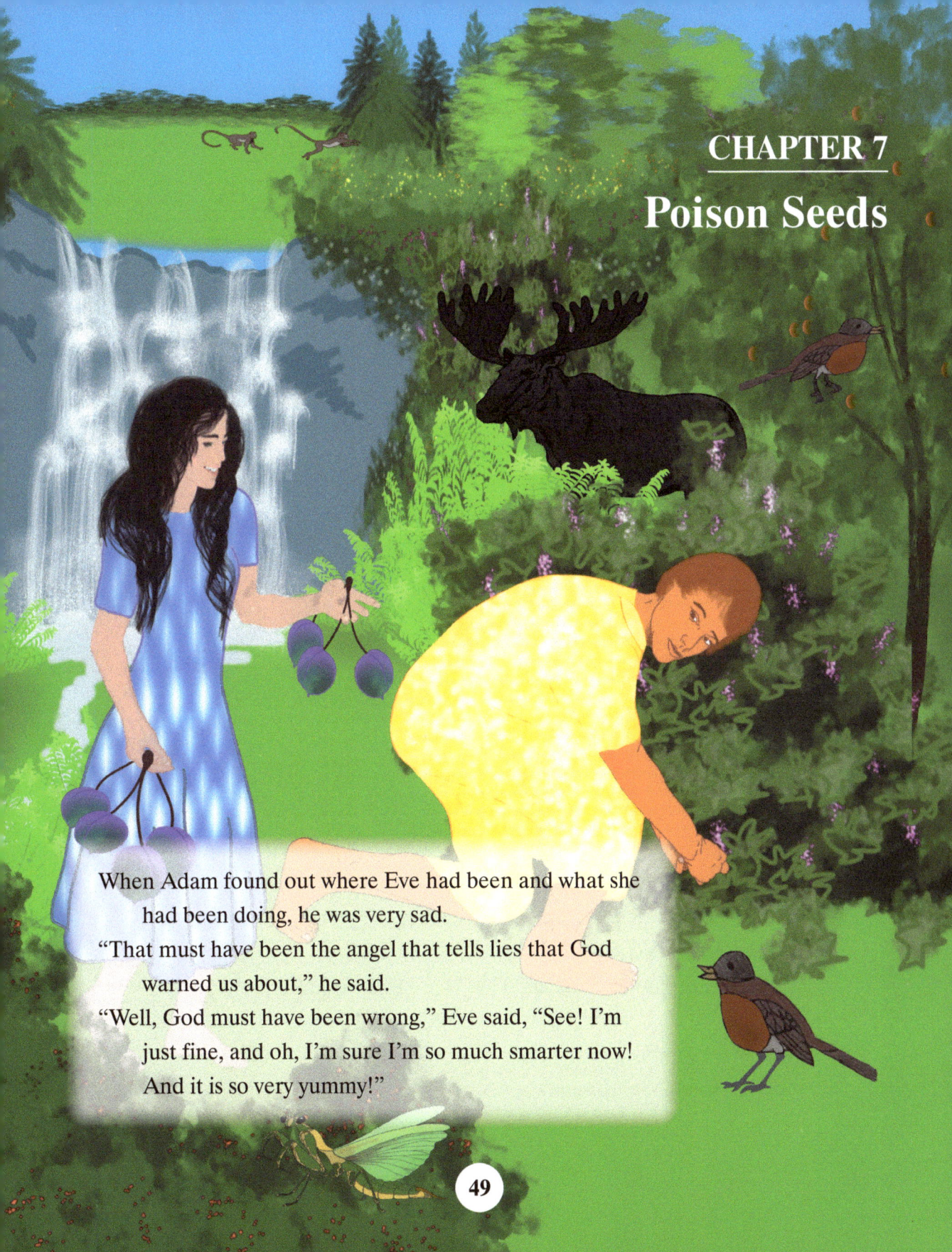

CHAPTER 7
Poison Seeds

When Adam found out where Eve had been and what she had been doing, he was very sad.

"That must have been the angel that tells lies that God warned us about," he said.

"Well, God must have been wrong," Eve said, "See! I'm just fine, and oh, I'm sure I'm so much smarter now! And it is so very yummy!"

Adam thought, "I love God, but I love Eve.
  Is God going to make Eve die?
  I don't want God to take Eve away from me.
  That doesn't seem fair!
  Maybe Eve is right anyway, and God won't make us die!"

So Adam chose to think poison ideas,
  and then he ate the fruit, too.

Then they remembered something even more scary!
God always came to visit them in the evening!
They didn't want Him to come visit them tonight.
What would happen when He came?
Would He be angry?
He would see them wearing big green leaves!
What would He do to them?
Would He make them die?

Being scared made them feel angry too.
"Why did you feed those fruits to me?" grumbled Adam.
"Why didn't you stay close like God told you to?"

God was so sad!
His friends had chosen to believe the poison lies.
He knew that the poison in those lies would grow up and kill them.

God had a plan. He knew what He was going to do.
But it wouldn't be easy, and it would take a long, long time.

God sadly went to the garden to talk to them.
He knew that they were very scared.
He knew that they were hiding.

"Where are you?" He called.
"I'm scared, and I'm hiding!" said Adam.
"And I don't have any clothes on."

"Why are you suddenly needing clothes?" God asked.
"Did you eat the fruit of the tree of knowing good and evil?"

That means that you don't believe anymore that I really love you. If knowing evil would make you smart or happy, I would never have asked you to stay away. It didn't make you happy, did it?"

"It's all Eve's fault, and You made her," Adam said.
"What did you do?" God asked Eve.
"It's all the snake's fault, and You made the snake," Eve said.

"Oh, Snake," God said. "You were given beautiful shiny wings, and now you have done something very ugly. From now on, you won't have those wings anymore."

Then God talked to Satan who was really truly the one talking in the tree.

"People have chosen your poison ideas that I don't really love them, but one Person will come and change all of that. This will make you angry, and you will hurt Him. But eventually, all the poison seeds you've planted will be destroyed."

Adam and Eve had been listening closely!
What did it all mean?

CHAPTER 9
God Has a Plan

It had been a long, sad day. Adam and Eve had chosen to think poison thoughts, and eat the fruit of the tree of knowing good and evil. The poison ideas had already taken away their beautiful light clothes and had made them scared and angry and sad. They couldn't fix anything.

God had come to explain some things to them. They waited to hear what God was going to say now.

"Thinking that I don't really love you is a terribly poisonous seed. That kind of thinking makes you scared and angry, and not happy at all! It works inside you to kill you.

For now, you have to leave the garden, and the poison thought that you chose to think today, will eventually make you die. Being dead means that you don't move or think anymore. It's like being asleep with no dreams, and only Jesus can wake you up.

I gave you a beautiful world. Eating the fruit was like opening a door, and now Satan and his angels can go everywhere to tell you his poison ideas.
These poison seeds will also change the plants and animals.
Some plants will grow thorns.
Some animals will become mean.

This poison is called sin, and it can't be fixed right now, because there is so much you don't understand.

But I have a plan.

I will let the sin poison that you chose today kill me instead of you.

You will still have to die, but it won't be forever.

In fact, anyone who wants to can choose to let me take their sin poison away. Then I can wake you up from being dead, and you can live and be happy again.

I will do it all for you because I really do love you.
I want to do this for you.
You can again choose to believe that I love you."

Jesus really does love you.
He came and never chose to think poison thoughts.
He really did come and let our sin poison kill Him.
He did it all because He wanted to,
— because He wants to be able to wake us up from being dead so that we can live and be happy forever instead.

We have had sin poison thoughts too. But just like Adam and Eve did, we can choose again, and know that God really, truly loves us. Then we can thank Jesus for letting our sin poison kill Him instead of us.

CHAPTER 10
Adam and Eve Learn About the Lamb

God loves us very much. When people choose to believe that God doesn't really love them, they are believing a lie. That thought is so very poisonous, that if we choose to think like that, it will make us do something selfish. God names that "sin." Then it makes us die forever.

God knows that sometimes we get tricked into thinking sin thoughts, and doing something selfish. We think that it will make us happy. He doesn't want us to die forever. He wants us to have another chance to really know that He loves us.

God made a plan.
If we decided that we wanted another chance,
If we wanted to stop thinking poisonous sin thoughts,
If we really wanted to stop doing selfish things, He would take them away—
But only if we really wanted Him to.

He would have to become just like us and live down here without ever thinking sin thoughts even one time—without ever doing one thing that was selfish. No matter what would happen, He would always choose to believe that God loved Him. He would take all of our sin poison inside Himself, and that would make Him die.

He would do that just because He loves us so much.

But how could He explain it so people could understand that poisonous sin thoughts make us die? How could He explain that He had made another chance? How could He explain what He was going to do, and how much He loves us?

How could people show that they really wanted to stop thinking sin thoughts,
That they really wanted to stop doing selfish things,
That they really wanted Him to take all those things away?
God thought of a way that would help us choose.

God told Adam and Eve how they could show that they wanted to choose God's plan.
They needed to find a little lamb.
A little lamb is sweet and loving—just like God.
They needed to say that they were sorry for the selfish things they did and the poisonous sin thoughts they had.

Then they had to let the little lamb take this sin, just like Jesus would.

They had to kill the little lamb, just like their sin was going to kill Jesus.

They would pile up rocks, and burn up the little lamb on top just like all sin thoughts and selfish things will be burnt up.

They would do this to show that they believed that Jesus was going to come and do all of this for them. Jesus would be the Wonderful God Lamb.

Have you ever thought a poisonous thought that made you do something selfish? Do you remember how you felt after? God explains that awful feeling. He calls it burning.

When we ask Him to, He takes those poisonous things away so that they don't burn us up inside. He calls that forgiving. He gives us another chance and we let Him take our sin poison.

CHAPTER 11
Cain and the Lamb

Adam and Eve did just what God said. They were very happy that God had made a plan to save them from the poisonous sin thoughts and from doing selfish things.
Adam and Eve had lots and lots of children.
As their children grew up, they taught them all about how good God was.

They carefully told them all about what had happened in the garden.
They told them about the angel who tells lies,
 and wants them to think that God doesn't love them.
They taught them all about how terrible it feels to have poisonous sin thoughts
 inside.
They told them about God's wonderful plan to give them another chance to choose.
They taught them how to show that they wanted Jesus to save them too.

But one boy didn't think that God was good at all.
He thought, "Why did God make us leave the pretty garden?"
"Why did He let the earth start to make thorns and thistles?"
"Why am I supposed to do everything exactly as He says?"
"Why does He make everything so hard?"
"God isn't fair!"
The boy's name was Cain.

Cain grew up. His favorite thing to do was to work with the pretty, growing plants. One day he thought, "I don't know why I have to find a lamb as God said."
"Why does He have to have a lamb?"
"He should be happy with whatever I decide to give Him."

Was that right? Did God need lambs killed? Did that make God happy?
No! We needed the clear picture of how ugly and poisonous sin is.
We needed to see what God wants to do for us.
    How He was coming to be the Wonderful God Lamb.
We needed to remember how much He loves us.

It makes God happy when we see that He loves us so much.
It makes Him happy when we choose to let Him take away our poisonous sin thoughts and the selfish things we do.
It makes Him happy to know that He will wake us up again if we die.

CHAPTER 12
Dangerous Thoughts

Cain had been thinking some dangerous thoughts.
He and his brother each brought an offering to the garden gate for God.
Cain decided to make God happy by giving God some fruit that he had grown.
Cain's brother decided to obey God and choose to let God take away his poisonous sin thoughts.

God showed Cain that it wasn't the presents that made Him happy. It was being able to save him from poisonous sin thoughts! That made Cain angry.

"God is good and fair," Cain's brother said. "He loves you too!"
That made Cain even more angry!
God came to talk to Cain.
"Be careful, Cain," God said, "you are thinking very dangerous thoughts!"

But Cain didn't listen.
He got so angry that he killed his brother.

"Cain! What did you do?" God said.
"I don't know what happened to him," Cain said.

"Oh, Cain," God said, "when you killed your brother, that added even more sin poison on earth. That poison has hurt the earth, and now it will be even harder for the pretty plants to grow that you love so much!"

"Because you are not wanting me to take away the poisonous sin thoughts inside of you, the burning feeling will make you go far away. It won't let you live at home anymore."

Cain was not happy about what the sin poison had done.
He thought God had made the plants harder to grow.
He thought God had made the ugly, burning feelings inside of him.
He was angry at God.
He decided to move as far away from God as he could. He decided to live far away from anybody that loved God.

Cain was the first person on earth who didn't want to ever believe that God loved him. He chose the very same thoughts that had made Satan leave heaven. Those thoughts made Cain leave his home and family too. Satan had told lies to the angels. Some angels believed him, and left heaven with him. Cain told those same lies to his family, and some of them believed him and left home with him too.

God doesn't make the poison that hurts our world, or burns inside us.
He doesn't need us to give Him presents to make Him happy with us.
He really loves us.
God wants us to be really happy.
He wants to fix all the things that make us unhappy.

Jesus came and did everything that God promised.
He gave us a much better picture of how ugly and poisonous sin is.
He gave us a much better picture of how much God loves us.
Now we don't need to find a lamb, because Jesus was our Lamb—
our Wonderful God Lamb.

We can pray and tell Jesus, "I want You to take my poison sin thoughts away. I don't want to do selfish things anymore. I know that You really do love me.
Thank you for loving me all the time."

CHAPTER 13
Dangerous Choosing

Adam and Eve's children all grew up.
Their grandchildren all grew up.
Their great-grandchildren all grew up.
Some of them knew that God loved them.
They would come to the gate of the garden to be as close to God as possible.

But, some of them thought that Satan was right.
They moved away so nobody would try to tell them what to do.
Then they had children who grew up too.
More and more people lived on earth.
More and more people didn't want God or His rules anymore.

Because God loved everyone, He let them all be free to choose what to think.

Satan was so pleased!
He told God, "You have to leave Earth alone now because all the people are on my side."

God said, "I love every person on Earth. I love Earth, too.
I take care of everything and keep everything safe.
I don't want to leave them all alone.
Then there won't be anyone to take care of them."

Enoch was a person that knew that God loved them.
He went to visit the cities.
The people there didn't know that God's rules would help them to be happy. They didn't know that God loved them.
Only a few people listened.

God knew that something very bad would happen.
Everything on Earth was safe because God was taking care of it.
If God's good laws stopped even for a blink,
    all the water that He had put in different places
      would try to come back together again.
That would be a flood that would drown everything.

God loved everyone.
How could He save all the people that still loved Him?
How could He still let the others be free to choose?
How could He save Earth?

CHAPTER 14
Noah Helps

God had a plan.
He knew how He could save everyone who would
 choose to listen.
He knew of a family that would help.

"Noah," God said,
"I can see that something very bad is going to happen.
The water is not going to stay where I put it.
It will drown everything."
"What can I do to help?" Noah asked.

God said, "You need to build a boat that is big enough so that everybody that chooses to, can be saved.
You will need to put enough food in the boat to last a long time.
And you need to tell everyone about the flood that is coming."

God told Noah how to build the boat.
Because it was a special boat that would save people, God named it the Ark.
He told Noah how big it should be so that He could save everyone.

Noah told his family what God had said.
"We'll help," they promised.

Noah and his family started to build the ark.
It was a very big boat.
Building it took a very long time!
Getting all the food took a very long time.

Noah told everyone about the flood that was coming.
Most people didn't want to think about God.
They did experiments to try to prove a flood could never happen.
Then they stopped listening to Noah's warning.

One day, God told Noah, "Most people won't listen. Let's use the extra room to save all the different kinds of animals."

God's good angels helped by leading all the different kinds of birds and animals in a big parade. Only two of most kinds of animals and birds could come. A few special kinds could have seven saved.
Everyone watched. This had never happened before!

"Oh," thought Noah, "they will listen now."
He came and told them again that they could choose to be saved.
Nobody came.
Sadly, Noah and his family went into the ark.
Sadly, a good angel shut the big door.

Noah and his family and all the different kinds of birds and animals were safe, but so many people were outside!

The people outside were not sad. They laughed and laughed! "Silly old Noah got locked in his zoo!"

CHAPTER 15
God Looks Away

Noah and his family waited patiently inside the ark.
The people outside laughed and laughed.
They decided to have a big party about the silly old man Noah!

A week later, someone saw something very strange in the sky!
What was it?

Nobody had ever seen clouds before.
And now there were so many!
Something was falling!
What was it?
Nobody had ever seen rain before.
It fell faster and faster.
Maybe Noah was right! But they
   didn't want to think about it.
Maybe it would go away.

But it didn't. It got worse!
Every day when they woke up, they would look outside and say, "It's still raining!"
The water got deeper and deeper.
Finally, people started to be really scared. They went to the ark.
"Hey Noah, let us in!" they shouted.
But Noah couldn't open the door.

They decided to move to the highest places they could.
All the animals decided that too.
The water kept getting deeper and deeper.
Finally, everything on Earth was covered in water.
There was nothing to stop the great big waves.

The storm was so terrible
    that even Satan and his angels were scared.
They wished that they hadn't told God to leave Earth alone.
They couldn't keep it safe!

God sent His good angels to keep the ark safe
    as it tumbled around in the storm.
The good angels weren't afraid.
They knew that God was with them and would
keep them safe.

God made sure that as the Earth broke,
parts of land would poke up high.
He made sure that there were deep places for the water to go.
The big storm stopped.

Then He sent a big wind to dry up the extra water.
The water dried up around the ark.
It dried up underneath the ark.
The plants started to grow again.

There would never be another flood covering Earth now.
But Noah didn't know that.
Finally, the Earth was dry enough.
The plants were big enough.
God told Noah to let all the animals out of the ark.

Noah and his family were very happy that God loved them.
They were very happy that God had saved them.
"Thank you, God," they prayed.
But they were still scared.
What a strange wild world it was!

God knew that they were still afraid.
He showed them a beautiful rainbow.
"I promise that this will never happen again," God said.
"We will look at the rainbow together, and remember that I love you."

God loves us so much, that He won't ever leave us.
His rules keep us all happy and keep us close to God.

But He loves us enough to let us go away from Him if we choose to.
We are never safe away from God.

God tells us,
"I am the One who goes ahead of you to keep you safe.
I will stay with you all the time.
I will not go away. I will not leave you alone.
So don't be scared.
Don't be afraid.

Deuteronomy 31:8

CHAPTER 16

A Bad, Bad Trick

One day, God decided to have a meeting. Satan decided to go too.

"I rule the world!" Satan said.
 "Everybody is on my side."

"Really?" God said! "What about My good
 friend Job?"
"Job loves Me.
Job is nice to his family.
Job is nice to everyone."

Satan did not want to admit that Job loved God.
He told God, "He just pretends to love You
 because You give him so many nice things!"
God said, "Prove it!"

But that wasn't all!
Then He told Job's friends that God had hurt Job's animals and Job's workmen, and Job's children.
Job's friends believed that God made the big hurting sores that were all over Job.

Job's friends came to visit Job.
They said, "Job, you must be a very bad man. God only hurts bad people."
Job did not know what to think.
Was God hurting him?
He hadn't done anything bad!

What a bad, bad trick.
Satan laughed and laughed. Ha! Ha!
    Ho! Ho! Ho!
      Hee! Hee! Hee!
Then Satan stopped laughing.
Why?

God was coming!
God came down to talk with Job.
He told Job that his friends were wrong.
He said, "I am not like that."

God said, "You weren't around in the very beginning,
    so there are things that you don't understand.

Where did good and bad come from?

Look at the big dragon[2] that lives in the water. He is so strong that it seems like he can do anything he wants to. Who is going to stop him? Even though I made him, he has decided to be mean and hurt others.
This is a picture to think about, because it will help you understand."

---

[2]*Isa. 27:1 tells us that the dragon that lives in the seas is also called leviathan. Ps. 104:26 tells us that God made leviathan. In Job 41:18–21 God describes leviathan as a fire-breathing dragon that lives in the sea. Before 1841 dinosaurs were drawn and called dragons, which is a word that means "terrible lizard."*

"Everything I created has a choice to be loving and kind, or not. Some creatures that I have created have chosen not to, and some of them are very strong and powerful. Sometimes they choose to hurt and destroy others."

"I am not like that, and I will never change and be like that.
I choose to treat everyone as my friend because I really do love them!"

I am so glad that God told Job that He is not like that, because Satan still tries that same bad trick now.
He figures out a way to hurt somebody and make them sad.
Did he do this to you?

Then Satan has a great big laugh. Ha! Ha!
    Ho! Ho! Ho!
    Hee! Hee! Hee!

We invite you to view the complete
selection of titles we publish at:
www.TEACHServices.com

We encourage you to write us
with your thoughts about this,
or any other book we publish at:
info@TEACHServices.com

TEACH Services' titles may be purchased in
bulk quantities for educational, fund-raising,
business, or promotional use.
bulksales@TEACHServices.com

Finally, if you are interested in seeing
your own book in print, please contact us at:
publishing@TEACHServices.com

We are happy to review your manuscript at no charge.

www.ingramcontent.com/pod-product-compliance
Lightning Source LLC
Chambersburg PA
CBHW040927240426
43667CB00024B/2979